CW00730057

Fighting Corruption and Sin

by
Jorge Cardinal Bergoglio
(Pope Francis)

*All booklets are published thanks to the
generous support of the members of the
Catholic Truth Society*

CATHOLIC TRUTH SOCIETY
PUBLISHERS TO THE HOLY SEE

Contents

ISBN 978 1 86082 875 1

Preface

In meetings with archdiocesan and civil organisations in our city, the theme of corruption, as one of life's ongoing factors, keeps coming up. You hear about people and institutions that are visibly corrupt and that have begun to decompose, losing their identity, their capacity to exist, to grow, to approach fulfilment, to serve the whole of society. This is nothing new: ever since the birth of mankind, this phenomenon has always existed. Clearly, it is a process of death - when life dies, there is corruption. I often notice that people talk about corruption and sin as though they were identical, which is not really true. A situation of sin and a state of corruption are two different things, though closely interrelated.

Corruption: "denounced but acceptable"

With this in mind, I thought it would be appropriate to republish an article I wrote in 1991. At that time the media were giving a lot of space and time to this topic. It was the time when the Catamarca affair was polarising the nation's attention, and many people were astonished that such things could happen.[1] Then we started getting used to the word "corruption" and to the fact of it, as if it were just part of daily life. We know that we are all sinners, but the new thing that has now entered the collective imagination is that corruption seems to be part of the normal life of society, an aspect of citizenship that is denounced but acceptable. I don't want to go into details: the newspapers are full of them.

Discerning corruption

Our archdiocese is holding an assembly. We cannot ignore this theme which, as I said, comes up in our talks and meetings. It will do us good to reflect together on this problem and also on its relationship with sin. It will do us good to shake up our souls with the prophetic force of the Gospel, which places us in the truth about things by stirring up the layers of fallen dead leaves from which human weakness and complicity create the leaf mould that nurtures corruption. It will do us a lot of good, in the light of God's word, to learn to discern the different states of corruption that surround us and threaten to lead us astray. It will do us good to say to one another again, "Yes, I'm a sinner; but no, I'm not corrupt!" - and to say it with fear, lest we accept the state of corruption as just another sin.

The beauty of redemptive humility

"Yes, I'm a sinner." How beautiful it is to be able to feel and say this, and by doing so to plunge into the mercy of the Father who loves us and is waiting for us at every moment. "Yes, I'm a sinner," as the publican said in the temple ("God, be merciful to me, a sinner!" *Lk* 18:13); as Peter felt and said, first in words ("Leave me, Lord; I am a sinful man," *Lk* 5:8), and later in tears, when he heard the cock crow that night, a moment that the genius of J S Bach captured in the sublime aria *Erbarme dich, mein Gott* (Have mercy, my God). "Yes, I'm a sinner," as Jesus teaches us that the prodigal son said: "I have sinned against heaven and against you" (*Lk* 15:21) - and could not go on, because he was enfolded in his waiting father's loving embrace. "Yes, I'm a sinner," as the Church has us say at the beginning of Mass and every time we look at our crucified Lord. "Yes, I'm a sinner," as David said when the prophet Nathan opened his eyes with his forceful truth-telling (*2 S* 12:13).

Corruption is not open to this beauty

But how difficult it is for the force of truth to shatter hearts that are corrupt! They are so wrapped up in their self-sufficiency that they admit no questioning. A corrupt person is one who "stores up treasure for himself in place of making himself rich in the sight of God" (*Lk* 12:21). They feel comfortable and happy, like the man who was planning to build new barns (*Lk* 12:16-21), and if the situation becomes difficult, they know all the excuses to get themselves out of it, like the corrupt steward (*Lk* 16:1-8), an early practitioner of the philosophy of "if you don't steal it's because you aren't clever enough". Corrupt people are those who have built up their self-esteem based on that type of deceitful attitude, and go through life taking the shortcuts of self-advantage, at the price of their own true dignity and other people's. Their expression is constantly one of "it wasn't me," with faces as innocent as a holy picture, as my grandmother used to say. They could be awarded honorary doctorates in social cosmetics. And the worst of it is that they end up believing themselves. How difficult it is for any word of truth to find its way into their hearts! Therefore, though we say "Yes, I'm a sinner," let's shout aloud: "but no, I'm not corrupt!"

The corrupt do not face up to the truth

One of the characteristics of corrupt people when faced with truth-telling is that they can never allow themselves to be called into question. At the first sign of criticism they react angrily, deny the right of the person or institution to pass judgement on them, try to refute any moral authority that dares to question them; they have recourse to sophistries and semantic equivocations, belittle others and hurl insults at anyone who thinks differently (cf. *Jn* 9:34). Corrupt people generally berate themselves unconsciously, and then project the irritation produced by this self-blame onto others, so that they turn from attacking themselves to attacking others.

Evidence in the Gospel

St Luke shows the fury of these men (cf. *Lk* 6:11) on hearing the truth spoken by Jesus: "they were furious, and began to discuss to the best way of dealing with Jesus." They persecute others by imposing a rule of terror on all those who oppose them (cf. *Jn* 9:22) and get their revenge by expelling them from their society (cf. *Jn* 9:34-35). They are afraid of the light because their souls have become like earthworms, dwelling in darkness, underground. In the Gospel we see corrupt people twisting the truth, laying traps for Jesus (cf. *Jn* 8:1-11; *Mt* 22:15-22; *Lk* 20:1-8), plotting to get rid of him (cf. *Jn* 11s:45-57), bribing someone to betray him (cf. *Mt* 26:14-16) or bribing the soldiers on guard (cf. *Mt* 28:11-15). St John sums them up in a single phrase: "a light that shines in the dark, a light that darkness could not overpower [or 'grasp']" (*Jn* 1:5). These are men who cannot grasp the truth. We can re-read the Gospels looking for the typical features of these people, and their reaction to the light brought by Our Lord.

Being alert to the dangers of corruption

In offering this booklet to the public once more, I hope, in this time of the diocesan assembly, that it will prove useful to help us understand the danger of personal and social collapse that corruption brings; and that it will also help us to be vigilant, because a habitual state of everyday complicity with sin can lead us to corruption. The season of Advent is an appropriate time for us to be alert for anything that prevents us from opening our hearts to the desire of meeting Jesus Christ when he comes. May we allow ourselves to encounter him in order to journey afresh along the path of Christian life.

I would like to thank Father Gustavo O Carrara in particular for his moral support in producing this publication.

Cardinal Jorge Mario Bergoglio, SJ
Buenos Aires, 8th December 2005
Solemnity of the Immaculate Conception

Reflections on the Subject of Corruption

These days there is a lot of talk about corruption, especially with regard to politics.[2] The phenomenon is denounced in various sectors of society. Several bishops have pointed to the "moral crisis" currently experienced by many institutions. At the same time, there has been a growing general reaction to certain events whose origins lie in corruption, and in some cases, like the Catamarca affair, given the apparent inability to find a normal solution to the problem, public action took the form of demonstrations bordering on a new Fuenteovejuna.[3] It is a time when the reality of corruption is being brought very noticeably to light.

Getting to the roots of corruption

And yet all corruption at the social level is simply the result of a corrupt heart. There would be no social corruption if there were no corrupt hearts: "It is what comes out of a man that makes him unclean. For it is from within, from men's hearts, that evil intentions emerge: fornication, theft, murder, adultery, avarice, malice, deceit, indecency, envy, slander, pride, folly. All these evil things come from within and make a man unclean." (*Mk* 7:20-23).

When the human heart
does not have God as its treasure

A corrupt heart: this is where the problem lies. Why does
a heart become corrupt? For a human person, the heart is
not a dead end, closed on itself; it is not where the give-
and-take of relations (including moral relations) stops.
On the contrary, the human heart is a heart only insofar
as it can pass to something else, inasmuch it is capable
of attaching itself to others, inasmuch as it is capable of
loving or of denying love (which is hating). This is why
Jesus, when he invites us to see the heart as the source of
our actions, calls our attention to the ultimate direction
taken by our questing heart: "Where your treasure is,
there will your heart be also" (*Mt* 6:21). To know a man's
heart, to see what state it is in, necessarily involves finding
out the treasure towards which that heart is pointing:
the treasure that liberates and fulfils it, or that destroys
and enslaves it - or, in the case at hand, the treasure that
corrupts it. From the fact of corruption (whether personal
or social), then, we come to the human heart as originator
and maintainer of that corruption; and from the heart, we
come to the treasure to which that heart is attached.

Method

I would like to reflect on this fact so as to understand it better and also to help prevent "corruption" from becoming a mere commonplace, just another word, one of those that are used automatically, emptied of real meaning, by the relativist culture that uses language to reverse true values - the culture that tends to stifle the strength of the one Word. I think that in the first place it may help to get inside the internal structure of the state of corruption by "pondering the ugliness and malice that…it contains"[4], in the knowledge that, while corruption is a state that is intrinsically connected to sin, it is distinct from it. In the second place, it is also helpful to discover how a corrupt person, a corrupt heart (as distinct from a sinful person) acts. In the third place, we can go over some of the forms of corruption that Jesus had to face up to in his time.

The religious and corruption

Finally, it will help to ask ourselves about the type of corruption that might apply to a religious. Of course, a religious can carry within himself the same kind of corruption as other people, but here I would like to ask about what I would call "minor key" corruption: the possibility, that is, that a religious might have a heart that is corrupt, but (so to speak) only venially, meaning that his loyalties towards Jesus Christ were suffering from a kind of paralysis. Is it possible for a religious to be in some way "partially" or "venially" corrupt? All these things offer us, methodologically, different viewpoints from which to tackle the theme of corruption. In addition, we should note that "corruption" is a loaded word,[5] charged with contemporary meanings, and there is a risk of forcing our reflection off course to follow these.

Being Self-Contained

We should not confuse sin and corruption. Sin, especially repeated sin, leads to corruption, but not in a quantitative way (so many sins equals one corrupt person), but qualitatively, by creating habits that spoil and narrow the person's capacity to love, turning the heart's direction more and more towards goals that are close to its own self-containedness, its selfishness. As St Paul says: "For what can be known about God is perfectly plain to them since God himself has made it plain. Ever since God created the world his everlasting power and deity - however invisible - have been there for the mind to see in the things he has made. That is why such people are without excuse: they knew God and yet refused to honour him as God or to thank him; instead, they made nonsense out of logic and their empty minds were darkened. The more they called themselves philosophers, the more stupid they grew, until they exchanged the glory of the immortal God for a worthless imitation, for the image of mortal man, of birds, of quadrupeds and reptiles" (*Rm* 1:19-23). Here we see clearly the process that goes from sin to corruption, with all that this implies of blindness, turning away from God to rely on one's own efforts, etc.

Forgiveness

It would be fair to say that sins are forgiven, but corruption cannot be forgiven. This is simply because at the bottom of every corrupt attitude there is a weariness with the transcendent: instead of a God who never tires of forgiving, the corrupt person sets himself up as sufficient for his own salvation - and he gets tired of asking for forgiveness.

Self-sufficiency paralyses the heart

This is the first characteristic of all corruption: being self-contained. In the corrupt person there exists a basic self-sufficiency, which begins unconsciously, and afterwards becomes the most natural thing in the world. Human self-sufficiency is never an abstract thing. It is an attitude of the heart that is directed towards a "treasure" that seduces, tranquilises, and deceives it. "My soul, you have plenty of good things laid by for many years to come; take things easy, eat, drink, have a good time" (*Lk* 12:19). And curiously enough, a contradiction is set up: the self-sufficient person is basically a slave to that treasure, and the more enslaved he is, the more insufficient he feels in that very self-sufficiency.

A dangerous imbalance

This explains why corruption cannot stay hidden. The imbalance between the conviction of self-sufficiency and the reality of being enslaved to a treasure cannot be suppressed. It is an imbalance that forces its way out, boils over with its own pressure, and on emerging, gives off the stink produced by its confinement: it smells bad. Yes, corruption stinks of rottenness. When something begins to smell bad, it is because there is a heart stuck between its own self-contained self-sufficiency and the real impossibility of being enough for itself; it is a heart that has gone rotten by clinging too strongly to a treasure that has captured it.

The ignorance of the corrupt

Corrupt people do not notice their own corruption. It is the same as when someone has bad breath: they seldom realise it themselves. Other people can smell it, and need to tell them. Hence, also, it would be hard for someone who is corrupt to escape from that state through inner repentance. Their good spirit in this regard is anaesthetised. Generally, Our Lord saves them through means of trials that come from situations they experience (illness, loss of their money, loss of loved ones, etc.) and these are what pierce the armour of their corruption and enable grace to enter. Then they can be cured.

Appearances

From this it is apparent that corruption, rather than being forgiven, needs to be cured.[6] It is like one of those embarrassing illnesses that people try to disguise, and cover up until they can no longer be kept hidden. This at last opens up the possibility of being cured. Corruption should not be confused with vices (although familiarity with vices leads to making them into one's "treasure"). Corrupt people always try to keep up a good appearance: Jesus gives the name of "whitened sepulchres" to one of the most corrupt groups of his time (cf. *Mt* 23:25-28). Corrupt people cultivate their good manners to the point of fastidiousness, so as to cover up their evil habits.[7]

The appearance of being excusable

In the behaviour of a corrupt person, their sick attitude will appear merely as etiolated and will look, at worst, like weaknesses or weak points that are relatively admissible and excusable by society. For example, someone who is corrupted with ambition for power will seem, at most, to have a certain tendency to fickleness or superficiality that leads him to change his mind or adapt his behaviour depending on the situation; he will be called weak or adaptable or self-interested, but the wound of his corruption (ambition for power) will remain hidden. Another instance would be someone corrupted by lust or avarice, who disguises his condition in forms that are more socially acceptable, and appear to be mere pleasure-seeking and frivolity.

The gravity of frivolity

But frivolity is in fact a much graver sin than lust or avarice, simply because the frivolous person has permanently set his sights on a short-range objective in a way that is reversible only with great difficulty. Sinners, on recognising themselves as such, in some way admit the falseness of the treasure that they were or are attached to, whereas the corrupt person has put his vice through a crash course in good manners; he conceals his true treasure not by hiding it from other people's eyes but by refashioning it to be socially acceptable.[8] And their self-sufficiency grows: it begins with fickleness and frivolity, and ends up in the conviction, the absolute certainty, that they are better than anyone else:

> He spoke the following parable to some people who prided themselves on being virtuous and despised everyone else, 'Two men went up to the Temple to pray, one a Pharisee, the other a tax collector. The Pharisee stood there and said this prayer to himself, "I thank you,

God, that I am not grasping, unjust, adulterous like the rest of mankind, and particularly that I am not like this tax collector here. I fast twice a week; I pay tithes on all I get." The tax collector stood some distance away, not daring even to raise his eyes to heaven; but he beat his breast and said, "God, be merciful to me, a sinner". This man, I tell you, went home again at rights with God; the other did not. For everyone who exalts himself will be humbled, but the man who humbles himself will be exalted.' (*Lk* 18:9-14)

Making Comparisons

"...Particularly that I am not like this tax collector," because corrupt people constantly need to compare themselves to others who seem to be consistent in their lives (even when it is the consistency of the tax collector in confessing that he was a sinner) so as to cover up their own inconsistency, and justify their own attitude. To a fickle person, for example, someone who tries to hold on to clear, non-negotiable moral principles is a fundamentalist - old-fashioned, narrow-minded, someone who fails to keep up with the times. And here we see another typical trait of corrupt people: the way in which they justify themselves.

A need for justification

This is because, deep down, corrupt people feel the need to justify themselves, even though they don't actually realise what they are doing. The way that corrupt people justify themselves (i.e. justifying themselves by comparison with others) has two characteristics. In the first place, it is done with reference to situations that are extreme, exaggerated, or bad in themselves: rapaciousness, injustice, adultery, not fasting, not paying tithes (as in the above parable). They make reference to something exaggerated or to an undeniable sin and, in that context, set up a comparison between the good manners of their own faults and the severity of the sin to which they refer. The comparison is false, because its terms are of two different kinds: an appearance is compared to a reality. But at the same time they apply to the other person a reality that is not so straightforward.

Caricatures

And here we have their second characteristic: in any comparison, the other person is usually caricatured. Either the person himself is caricatured (as in the case of the Pharisee referring to the tax collector), or else there is a caricature in the connections that are made with external situations, or situations that affect him in some way, through the use of interpretations of facts in the light of other similar facts that are only apparently real, or that are real but wrongly applied. (That is the case of the Pharisees' insult to Jesus: "*We* were not born of prostitution;"[9] or the way they reduced Jesus's actions to those of a mere rebel: "If you set him free, you are no friend of Caesar's; anyone who makes himself king is defying Caesar."[10] Here, for example, a political note is projected into the comparison.) When we meet justifications of this kind, we can usually assume that what we are faced with is a case of corruption.

From Comparison to Judgement

On making such comparisons, corrupt people set themselves up in judgement over others: they themselves are the measure of morality.[11] "I am not like this tax collector" means "He is not like me, and I thank you for it."[12] As if to say, "I am the measure of how to fulfil the law: I pay tithes" etc. But in thus setting themselves up as the measure of all things, there is an underlying danger: no one can twist reality so much without running the risk of that same reality turning against them.

And from Judgement to Brazen Audacity

And it does turn against them. Being is transcendentally *verum*, true, and I can twist it and wring it like a towel, denying the truth; but being will continue to be true, even though in the context of a particular situation, someone manages to present it otherwise. Being fights to show itself as it is.[13] At the very heart of the judgement made by a corrupt person, there is set up a lie: a lie about life, a metaphysical lie about being, that in time will turn against the person who made it. On the moral plane, corrupt people avoid this by projecting their evil onto others. But this is merely a temporary solution, which only increases the tension of being towards the recovery of its truthfulness (since it never actually lost its truth). And Jesus tells the corrupt that the evil one is not the other person, but that "your eye is diseased".[14]

The loss of modesty

Corruption leads to the loss of the modesty that guards the truth, and that makes it possible for the truth to be truthful. It is modesty that, as well as the truth, guards the goodness, beauty and unity of being. Corruption works on a different plane from modesty: situating itself on this side of transcendence, it necessarily goes beyond in its pretentiousness and complacency. It has travelled the road all the way from modesty to acceptable shamelessness.[15]

Triumphalism

As well as being the measure of justice, there is yet another aspect. All corruption grows and at the same time expresses itself in an atmosphere of triumphalism. Triumphalism is the perfect breeding-ground for corrupt attitudes, because experience tells people that those sorts of attitudes produce good results, and so they feel like winners, triumphant. Everything works out well. And feeling good, being on a roll, they rearrange and reinforce situations with false evaluations.

A false optimism

That is not triumph but triumphalism. Fickleness and frivolity, for example, are forms of corruption that can germinate comfortably in the dire atmosphere of what Henri de Lubac calls "spiritual worldliness",[16] which is quite simply triumph mutated into triumphalism of the human capacity: pagan humanism subtly transformed into Christian common sense. Corrupt people, when integrating into their characters stable situations of the degeneration of being, do it in such a way that these situations encourage an optimistic feeling about their lives, to the extent that they are intoxicated with the anticipated eschatology that is triumphalism. Corrupt people have no hope. Sinners hope for forgiveness; but corrupt people don't, because they do not feel that they are in sin: they feel that they have triumphed. Christian hope has been reduced to the future possibility of a triumph that has already been achieved, as its inherent possession.[17]

The shifting of parameters

This triumphalism, born of feeling that one is the measure of all justice and judgement, gives itself airs and reduces everyone else to the measure of its own triumph. To put it another way: an atmosphere of corruption, a corrupt person, does not allow anyone to grow freely. Corrupt people know nothing of fraternity or friendship, only complicity. Loving one's enemies, or even the "friends/ enemies" distinction that was at the basis of the old law, are meaningless to corrupt people. Their parameters are different: for them, you are either accomplice or enemy. For example, when a corrupt person is in power, he will always implicate others in his own corruption, bring them down to his measure and make them accomplices of his chosen style.[18]

Corruption has its own proselytism

And all this is done in an atmosphere which is imposed on all: a triumphalist atmosphere, an atmosphere of "bread and circuses", with an appearance of common sense in judging things, and of practical feasibility in the different options. Since corruption includes the assumption of being oneself the measure of things, all corruption proselytises, pulls others in too. Sin and temptation are contagious, but corruption actively proselytises.[19]

"Enrolling" others in the state of corruption

This proselytising dimension of corruption points to its active nature and its skill in gathering others. It fits perfectly into the campaign plan of Lucifer, its leader, as presented by St Ignatius in the *Spiritual Exercises*.[20] The aim of gathering others is not to commit sins, but to enrol people in the state of sin, in the state of corruption: "nets and chains…first to tempt with a longing for riches …that men may more easily come to vain honour of the world [i.e. triumphalism], and then to vast pride." Its plan is to create a condition strong enough to resist the invitation to grace, both the "now" (the first type)[21] or the whole (the second type)[22].[23]

In Jesus's Time

In the New Testament we find corrupt people whose adherence to the state of sin is clear at a glance. Such is the case of Herod the Great[24] and Herodias.[25] In others, corruption is disguised as socially acceptable attitudes, for instance in the case of Herod Antipas who listened to John the Baptist and "liked to listen to him",[26] and opted for perplexity as a façade to defend his corruption; or Pilate, who acted as though the matter had nothing to do with him, and so washed his hands;[27] but underneath it all, he did so in order to defend his corrupt aim of clinging to power at all costs.

Corruption among the Jews of Jesus's time

But in Jesus's times there are also corrupt groups: the Pharisees, the Sadducees, the Essenes, the Zealots.[28] A look at these groups will help us to comprehend the fact of the corruption that opposed Jesus Christ himself, and his message of salvation. These four groups have two features in common. In the first place they have all drawn up a system of teaching to justify or cover up their corruption. The second feature: these groups go as far as they can to oppose, without actually declaring themselves the enemies of, sinners and the people. Not only do they consider themselves clean, but by that very attitude they proclaim their cleanliness.

Their complex corruption caused division

The Pharisees devise a system of teaching about how to fulfil the Law with an exaggerated degree of particular detail, and that leads them to despise sinners, whom they consider as breakers of this crushing law.[29] The Sadducees see sinners and the common people as small fry, unable to negotiate with power at the various junctures of life; and into their doctrine of negotiation with the ruling power, they put their own inner corruption, leaving no room for the hope that transcends this life. The Zealots seek a political solution, here and now. That is their teaching, and it conceals a large dose of social resentment and absence of a theological understanding of their times. For them, their people's theology of exile is no longer valid. And "the sinners", the common people, will end up as "useful idiots" whom they will summon to be indoctrinated into an armed struggle. Finally, at first glance it is difficult to see corruption in the Essenes, because they are men of very good will, who seek in monastic life recollection and salvation for a chosen group. Their corruption lies in this: they have been tempted under the appearance of good and have allowed that temptation to be consolidated as the doctrinal reference point for their lives. For them, sinners and the common people are outside that plan, and are unsuitable to swell the numbers of their group.

Jesus's response

The answer given by Jesus to John the Baptist is, over and above the Baptist himself, directed at them: "Go back and tell John what you have seen and heard: the blind see again, the lame walk, lepers are cleansed, and the deaf hear, the dead are raised to life, the Good News is proclaimed to the poor" (*Lk* 7:22).

Jesus stands, then, against these four groups, these four currents of corrupt doctrine, and recalls the promises of redemption made to his people.[30] He has recourse to the patrimony of his people, the Scriptures, as he did when he was tempted in the desert. He re-reads the Scriptures because it is they that bear witness to his style,[31] as against the alternative styles proposed by those four elites.

Summing Up

Corruption is not an act but a state, a personal and collective state, to which people get accustomed and in which they live. The values (or non-values) of corruption are integrated into a real culture, with a capacity for systematic doctrine, its own language, and its own particular way of acting. It is a culture of pygmyism, inasmuch as it gathers proselytes to bring them down to the level of admitted complicity.

A false and destructive culture

This culture has a dual dynamism: appearance and reality, immanence and transcendence. The appearance is not the breaking out of reality by way of truthfulness; it is the constructing of a reality in such a way that it can be imposed and accepted as widely as possible in society. It is a culture of taking away; reality is taken away and replaced by appearance. Transcendence becomes steadily more here-and-now, practically immanent; or, at most, an armchair transcendence. Being is no longer protected, but ill-treated through a kind of socially acceptable shamelessness. In the culture of corruption there is a lot of shamelessness, even though what is allowable in the corrupt atmosphere is fixed in severe, almost Victorian rules of conduct. As I said, it is a culture of good manners covering up evil habits. And that culture is imposed in the *laissez-faire* of everyday triumphalism.

Openness to forgiveness

People do not always become corrupt in one go. In fact, it is generally just the opposite. It is a slippery slope. And that slope is not always a clearly sinful path. It is possible for someone to be a great sinner and yet never to have fallen into corruption. That may have been the case of Zaccheus, Matthew, the Samaritan Woman, Nicodemus, and the Good Thief, who had something in their sinful hearts that saved them from corruption. The clinging to self-containment that is characteristic of corrupt people had not yet taken shape in them; they were still open to forgiveness. Their deeds were born of a sinful heart, many of them were evil deeds, but at the same time the heart that produced them could feel its own weakness. And that was where God's strength could find a way in. "God's foolishness is wiser than human wisdom, and God's weakness is stronger than human strength" (*1 Co* 1:25).

The path that leads to corruption is sin

I have been making a distinction, which may be dangerous, between sin and corruption; still, all in all, it is a true one. And yet it has to be said that the path that leads to corruption is sin. How so? It is a subtle kind of progression, or rather a qualitative leap from sin to corruption. The author of the Letter to the Hebrews tells us: "Be careful that no one is deprived of the grace of God and that no root of bitterness should begin to grow and make trouble; this can poison a whole community" (*Heb* 12:15). Obviously he is speaking here of something more than sin; he is pointing out a state of corruption. Ananias and Sapphira sinned, but it was not the sin of weakness of heart, but of corruption: they were cheating, trying to trick God,[32] and they were punished precisely because of the corruption created in them by their fraudulent action.

The wisdom of St Ignatius

Should we then start trying to tell the difference between sin and corruption? I don't think it would help much. What has been said up to now is quite enough. It is possible for someone to sin repeatedly and yet not be corrupt; but, at the same time, the repetition of sin can lead to corruption. St Ignatius understands this, and hence does not stop at knowledge of our own sins but takes us further, to knowledge and hatred of our disordered actions, and of all things that are worldly and vain.[33] He knows the danger of the "root of bitterness" that "makes trouble". For those doing the Spiritual Exercises, he seeks states of soul that are open to transcendence in their attachment to Our Lord; and that they should not keep any area of self-containment for themselves.

The Corruption of Religious

Corruptio optimi, pessima - the worst corruption is the corruption of the best. This can be applied to religious who are corrupt. They do exist. They existed in the past, as we can see from reading history. In the various religious orders that asked for reform or undertook it, the problem of corruption had been present to a greater or lesser extent. I don't want to talk here about obvious cases of corruption, but rather about everyday states of corruption, which I would call venial, but which bring the flow of religious life to a halt. How do these come about?

The closing of the soul

Blessed Peter Faber gave a golden rule for detecting the state of a soul that was living tranquilly and at peace: to propose to that person something *more* (*magis*).[34] The person whose soul was closed to generosity would react badly. The soul gets used to the bad smell of corruption. The same thing happens as in a closed space: only someone who comes in from outside notices the bad smell in the air. And when someone tries to help a person in that state, the amount of resistance is indescribable.

Moses fought corruption among the Israelites

The Israelites were slaves in Egypt, but they had got used to their loss of freedom, had adapted the shape of their souls to it, and had no ambition for any other way of living. Their consciences were asleep and, in that sense, we could say there was a certain degree of corruption. When Moses announced God's plan to the Israelites, "they would not listen to him, so crushed was their spirit and so cruel their slavery" (*Ex* 6:9). When difficulties came up over their escape from Egypt, they reproached Moses for having placed himself and them in that situation: "As they left Pharaoh's presence they met Moses and Aaron who were waiting for them. 'May the Lord see your work and punish you as you deserve!' they said to them. 'You have made us hated by Pharaoh and his court; you have put a sword into their hand to kill us'" (*Ex* 5:20-21).

Judith, Jonah and Elijah

Much later, the elders of Israel, tired and fearful, wished to make a pact with the enemy, and Judith had to come and re-read their history to them to stop them from accepting, like lambs condemned to slaughter, situations that were contrary to God's will.[35] Jonah wanted to avoid trouble: he was ordered to go to Nineveh and he set off for Tarshish,[36] and God had to intervene with a long purifying ordeal (a real night in the belly of the whale, a type of the night that lasted from the ninth hour of Good Friday to the dawn of the first day of the week). Elijah told himself that he had gone too far in the matter of slaughtering the priests of Baal, and he was overcome with fear of a woman (it reminds me of the Twelfth Rule of Discernment in the First Week of the *Spiritual Exercises*), and he took to flight and wished to die;[37] he was unable to bear the loneliness of a triumph in God.

The result of long suffering

Nathanael found it easier to say sceptically that nothing good could come from Nazareth[38] than to believe Philip's enthusiasm. The two disciples, like other Jonahs, also wanted to avoid trouble: they had been told to go to Galilee and they ran away to Emmaus;[39] and the rest of the Apostles preferred not to believe the evidence of their eyes in the Upper Room, and the Evangelist says that "their joy was so great that they still could not believe it" (*Lk* 24:41). That is the heart of the matter: a process of suffering always brings people down; the experience of defeat leads the human heart to become accustomed to it, so that people will not be surprised or suffer again if another one occurs. Or people simply content themselves with the state they are in, and do not want any more trouble.

A reluctance towards God

In all these Biblical references we find reluctance. The heart doesn't want any complications. People are afraid that God will get in and start them along paths that are beyond their control. They are afraid of God's visitation, afraid of his consolation. This engenders a sort of fatalism: their horizons become narrower to fit their loneliness or passivity. They are afraid of ambition and prefer the realism of less to the promise of something more, and forget that God's most real realism is expressed in a promise: "Leave your country, your family and your father's house, for the land I will show you. I will make you a great nation; I will bless you and make your name so famous that it will be used as a blessing" (*Gn* 12:1-2).

A subtle corruption

In the apparent realism of preferring less, a subtle process of corruption is already at work: people sink into mediocrity and lukewarmness (two forms of spiritual corruption), and into bargaining with God along the lines of the first and second "binaries" or types of people referred to above (p. 26 and notes 21-23). In penitential prayer, in the sacrament of reconciliation, they ask God for forgiveness for other sins; but they do not lay bare this disillusioned state of their soul before the Lord. This is the slow but fatal sclerosis of the heart.

"Religious consumerism"

Then the soul begins to satisfy its hunger with the products on offer in the supermarket of religious consumerism. More than ever, such people live the consecrated life as a self-contained fulfilment of their personalities.

Corruption closes the soul to transcendence

Many of them will find this self-fulfilment in job satisfaction, others in their success in works, others in the pleasure they get out of being highly regarded; others will seek by perfecting modern methods, to fill up the emptiness that their souls experience with respect to the final end that they once sought and allowed themselves to be sought by. Others will do it by leading an intense social life; they love going out, taking holidays with friends, attending lunches and receptions; they will try to be taken into account in everything that means cutting a figure in the world. I could go on listing cases of corruption; but, to simplify, all of that is only part of something deeper: the "spiritual worldliness" referred to above.[40]

Spiritual worldliness is paganism in an ecclesiastical disguise. In contrast with men and women who are corrupt in their consecrated life, the Church shows the greatness of her Saints, who have learned how to transcend all appearances, until they contemplate the face of Jesus Christ, and that has driven them "mad for Christ".[41]

Many men and women go through life in venial corruption, which clashes with their consecration; their souls lie by the pool, watching - for thirty-eight years - how the waters are stirred and others are cured.[42] Such hearts are corrupt. Someone there is daydreaming and wishing he could bring the dead part of his heart back to life; he hears the Lord's invitation… but no, it's too much trouble, too much like hard work. Our inner poverty needs to make a bit of an effort to open a space to transcendence, but the sickness of corruption holds us back: "*Ad laborem indigentia cogebat, et laborem infirmitas recusabat* - her poverty compelled her to work, and her sickness prevented her from working".[43] And Our Lord does not tire of calling, "Do not be afraid…" Don't be afraid of what? Don't be afraid of hope…and hope does not disappoint us.[44]

Endnotes

[1] Investigation of a notorious rape and murder in the Agentinian province of Catamarca in 1991 was hampered by the political authorities, whose family members appeared to be involved; this gave rise to widespread popular protest.

[2] Octavio Frigerio, 'Corrupción, un problema político,' *La Nación*, year 122, no. 42,863, Monday 4th March 1991, p. 7.

[3] For Catamarca, see the footnote to the Preface. In Fuenteovejuna, a village in Spain, in the fifteenth century, a cruel and tyrannical commander was murdered by a united band of the villagers, who were subsequently pardoned by the king; this was the subject of a play of the same name by Lope de Vega.

[4] *Spiritual Exercises* (henceforth *SE*), no. 57 (1st week, 2nd exercise, 2nd point).

[5] "*ein geladenes Wort*", as von Rad says.

[6] "Forgiven", "cured": the words are not accurate and not correct, because all forgiveness heals. I am setting them in opposition to each other here for the sake of helping us to understand the point.

[7] "Among these (partisan) directors there are some who, like the courtesans of old who acted as vestal virgins, try to escape suspicion (of being corrupt) today by officiating as unexpected guardians of the temple of public morality," Octavio Frigerio, op. cit.

[8] "Be careful not to parade your good deeds before men to attract their notice… do not have it trumpeted before you; this is what the hypocrites do…they love to say their prayers standing up in the synagogues and at the street corners for people to see them…do not put on a gloomy look" (*Mt* 6:1-16).

[9] *Jn* 8:39-41. Laurentin, discussing this text, cites some exegetes who think that it refers to the Mother of Jesus at the time when she returned to Nazareth from Ain Karim. Her pregnancy was apparent by that time, and this is what led Joseph to want to send her away in secret. Many people would have thought the worst, seeing her as having transgressed the Law. This exegesis is very possible from the biblical viewpoint - and now the Pharisees strike at the Mother of Jesus. I would see no difficulty in accepting that exegesis from the theological point of view, because it would mark still another step in Jesus's self-emptying, and that of his Mother, who accompanied him every step of the way.

[10] *Jn* 19:12. Obviously there is reductionism in this comparison.

[11] To set themselves up as judges, corrupt people try to present themselves as balanced, neither left-wing nor right-wing; and when circumstances compel them to adopt extreme measures that would denote their corruption, and show imbalance, they manage to prove that that imbalance was necessary for the sake of a higher order of balance. But never, even in tactical imbalance, do they cease to be the judge

of the situation. In this regard, see the comment by Frigerio quoted above: the very corruption of the courtesan turns her into a vestal virgin when it suits her.

[12] In other words, "I thank you that there are so few people like me." Corrupt people try to stand apart from any corporate group; they always feel they are beyond others.

[13] All creation is striving for this, as if with birthpangs, as St Paul says at *Rm* 8:22.

[14] *Mt* 6:23. And if it is evil, it would be better to pluck it out.

[15] Perhaps a comparison may help to understand this. Stealing a woman's purse is a sin, and the thief is sent to prison, and the woman tells her friends all about it, and everyone agrees that things are in a terrible state, and that the public authorities ought to do something about it, because it's not safe to go out. And the woman in question, who had her purse snatched, never even thinks about what her husband is like in business matters, how he cheats the State by not paying taxes, gets rid of his employees every three months to avoid dependency in employment relations, etc. And her husband, and perhaps she herself, boasts about these business tricks and underhand dealings. This is what I call acceptable shamelessness. Another instance: prostitution is a sin, and prostitutes are called "women of evil life" or simply "bad women". Socially they are reviled for contaminating culture and corrupting people, etc., etc. And the same person who says all that, goes to a party for the third marriage of a friend of theirs (after their second divorce), or accepts that so-and-so has a few "affairs" (provided that they are in good taste), or that this or that film star's love-life is published, when they change "partners" like a pair of shoes. What I am getting at is that there is a difference between the prostitute and the so-called "liberated" woman. The prostitute has not lost her shame; the other woman has gone beyond modesty and shame, and her attitude is one of shamelessness, which social convention makes acceptable.

[16] Henri de Lubac, *Meditations sur l'Eglise* (Paris, 1953) p. 327. Translated by Michael Mason as *The Splendour of the Church* (London, 1956).

[17] This phenomenon of the reduction of hope draws its strength from Joachim de Fiore's teaching about the "third Age". His concept of the Church was corrupted in that sense. Many systems of "immanent hope" were built up on his teaching. The mystery of the Church was thus re-read in the light of particular cultural movements or political events, and in that way a curious fact arose: in the name of progress, of taking a step forward in the development of mankind, transcendence was made into something self-contained, and that self-containment was actually a more dangerous kind of fundamentalism than the sort that involves a misunderstood return to the sources. It was the fundamentalism of immanence, of re-reading the mysteries of the Church in terms of political redemption or even in terms of political-cultural aspects of nations, however good these might be in themselves.

[18] It is no longer a measure with regard to value judgement, but also a measure of association or of reference to the coming together of adepts. To be fellow-soldiers with him, they have to be his accomplices.

[19] There are three characteristics of all temptation to sin: the temptation *grows*, it is *contagious* and it is *self-justifying*. These same characteristics also appear, but in a different way, in the state of corruption. Corruption is *consolidated*, *gathers others* and *establishes laws*. The *growth* of temptation now becomes a process of consolidation; the *contagiousness* of temptation becomes active proselytising; and finally, the simple *self-justification* of temptation is developed and worked up into established laws.

[20] *SE* 142 (Fourth Day, 3rd Point).

[21] *SE* 153 (Fourth Day, Meditation on three types of people, 1st type).

[22] *SE* 154 (Fourth Day, Meditation on three types of people, 2nd type).

[23] Here the reference is forced, because in the case of the binaries or types, it does not appear to be through corruption, but simply that something is acquired "not purely and duly for love of God" (*SE* 150; Fourth day, meditation on three types of people, 1st preamble). But it does serve as an example.

[24] *Mt* 2:3-15.

[25] *Mt* 14:3ff.; *Mk* 6:19.

[26] *Mk* 6:20.

[27] *Mt* 27:24.

[28] In this regard see Kurt Schubert, *Die jüdischen Religionsparteien in neutestamentlicher Zeit*. Here I simply give a very general and even simplified description of the matter, merely seeking to exemplify the case of the corruption of elites.

[29] *Mt* 23:13ff.

[30] Cf. *Is* 26:19; 42:7; 61:1.

[31] *Jn* 5:39.

[32] *Ac* 5:4.

[33] *SE* 63 (1st week, 3rd exercise, 1st colloquy).

[34] Blessed Peter Faber, *Memorial*, no. 151.

[35] *Jdt* 8:9ff.

[36] *Jon* 1:2-3.

[37] *1 K* 19:4.

[38] *Jn* 1:46.

[39] *Lk* 24:31.

[40] Spiritual worldliness is "the greatest danger, the most treacherous temptation, which is always reborn insidiously when all the others have been overcome and draws new strength from those very victories." Henri de Lubac, op. cit. De Lubac also defines it as "that which presents itself practically as a detachment from the other kind of worldliness, but whose moral and even spiritual ideal would be, instead of the glory of the Lord, man and his self-perfecting. Spiritual worldliness

is nothing other than a radically anthropocentric attitude. This attitude would be irremediable in the case - supposing it possible - of a man endowed with all spiritual perfections, who did not refer them to God. If that spiritual worldliness invaded the Church and worked to corrupt her by attacking her in her very principle, it would be infinitely more disastrous than any other merely moral worldliness. Worse still than the foul leprosy that, at certain moments in history, so cruelly disfigured the beloved Spouse, when religion appeared to set up scandal in the sanctuary itself, and, represented by a libertine Pope, hid the face of Jesus Christ under precious stones, cosmetics and spies… A subtle humanism that is the enemy of the Living God - and, secretly, no less the enemy of man - can install itself in us by a thousand subterfuges." *Ibid.*

[41] Peter-Hans Kolvenbach SJ, 'Locos por Cristo', *CIS (Review of Ignatian Spirituality)* XX, 1990, 1-2 (63-64), pp. 72-89. Also published in Kolvenbach, *Decir al indecible: estudios sobre los ejercicios espirituales de San Ignacio*, (Mensajero/ Sal Terrae 1999), pp. 115-132.

[42] *Jn* 5:5.

[43] St Augustine, addressing the Samaritan woman; *Tractates on the Gospel of John*, Tractatus 15 v. 17, *CCL*, 36, 156.

[44] *Rm* 5:5.

Spiritual Warfare

By Fr Vivian Boland OP

Every Christian is engaged in an ongoing struggle against the self, and against temptation, striving to gain the blessings of the Kingdom of God. This booklet enlightens the struggle by searching the wisdom of the scriptures. It gives hope to everyone, because Christ is always by our side to help us in every battle, and he has already defeated death and sin.

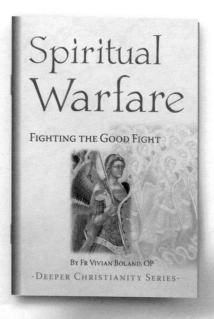

SP16   ISBN 978 1 86082 421 0

Pope Francis

By Dushan Croos SJ

In the brief time the newly elected Pope Francis spent on the balcony of St Peter's to greet his new diocese in Rome, many the world over were left asking who this man was who gave such a great impression of humility and approachability. This newly written biography tells the story of Jorge Mario Bergoglio's journey from modest beginnings in Buenos Aires, through his studies in chemistry to formation in the Society of Jesus, then as Archbishop in Buenos Aires and finally to the See of Peter.

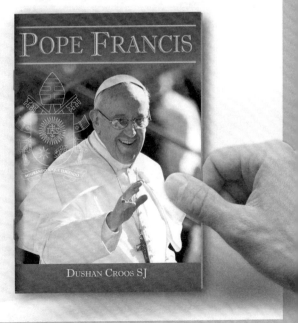

B752   ISBN 978 1 86082 870 6

Christian Love

By Fr John Edwards SJ

What does the Catholic Church teach on love and sex? Fr Edwards sets out a clear exposition of what love means in marriage, in chastity and in virginity. This booklet opens up clear thinking about the issues which, despite huge secular pressures to do so, just won't go away: contraception, pre-marital sex and homosexuality. It is an honest, engaging and straightforward "Catholic blueprint" for everyone – single, celibate or married – to aid them in seeing love for what it truly is: a gift, both human and divine, which is utterly beyond compare.

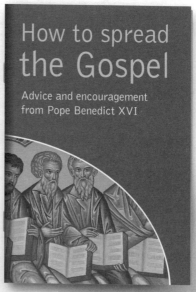

How to spread
the Gospel

Advice and encouragement
from Pope Benedict XVI

D0873 ISBN 978 1 86082 857 7

Desire and Delight

By Fr Robert Taylerson

Christianity is sometimes presented as a very glum affair, and the saints as killjoy ascetics who renounce all pleasure for the sake of virtue. Nothing could be further from the truth. Union with God gives happiness and delight, and God wills only our joy. This book examines the joys and pleasures of the Christian life through the Song of Songs and the Psalms.

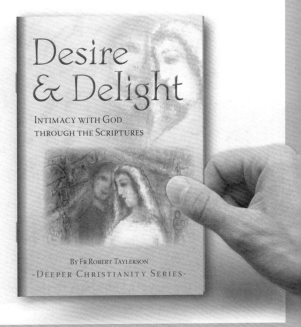

Desire & Delight

INTIMACY WITH GOD
THROUGH THE SCRIPTURES

BY FR ROBERT TAYLERSON
-DEEPER CHRISTIANITY SERIES-

SP40   ISBN 978 1 86082 869 0